Your Government:
How It Works

The House of Representatives

Daniel Partner

Arthur M. Schlesinger, jr.
Senior Consulting Editor

Chelsea House Publishers
Philadelphia

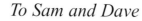

To Sam and Dave

CHELSEA HOUSE PUBLISHERS
Editor in Chief Stephen Reginald
Production Manager Pamela Loos
Art Director Sara Davis
Director of Photography Judy L. Hasday
Managing Editor James D. Gallagher
Senior Production Editor LeeAnne Gelletly

Staff for THE HOUSE OF REPRESENTATIVES
Project Editor Anne Hill
Project Editor/Publishing Coordinator Jim McAvoy
Associate Art Director Takeshi Takahashi
Series Designer Takeshi Takahashi, Keith Trego

The Chelsea House World Wide Web address is
http://www.chelseahouse.com

First Printing
1 3 5 7 9 8 6 4 2

Library of Congress Cataloging-in-Publication Data

Partner, Daniel.
    The House of Representatives / by Daniel Partner.
        p. cm. — (Your government—how it works)
    Includes bibliographical references and index.
    Summary: Surveys the history of the House of Representatives
and describes its structure, current function, and influence on
American society.
    ISBN 0-7910-5535-3 (hc)
    1. United States. Congress. House—Juvenile literature. 2. Leg-
islators—United States—Juvenile literature. [1. United States.
Congress. House. 2. Legislators. 3. United States—Politics and
government.] I. Title. II. Series.

JK1319 .P37 2000
328.73'072—dc21

99-048459

Contents

YOUR GOVERNMENT HOW IT WORKS

Introduction

Government: Crises of Confidence

Arthur M. Schlesinger, jr.

FROM THE START, Americans have regarded their government with a mixture of reliance and mistrust. The men who founded the republic understood the importance of government. "If men were angels," observed the 51st Federalist Paper, "no government would be necessary." But men are not angels. Because human beings are subject to wicked as well as to noble impulses, government was deemed essential to assure freedom and order.

The American revolutionaries, however, also knew that government could become a source of injury and oppression. The men who gathered in Philadelphia in 1787 to write the Constitution therefore had two purposes in mind: They wanted to establish a strong central authority and to limit that central authority's capacity to abuse its power.

To prevent the abuse of power, the Founding Fathers wrote two basic principles into the Constitution. The principle of federalism divided power between the state governments and the central authority. The principle of the separation of powers subdivided the central authority itself into three branches—the executive, the legislative, and the judiciary—so that "each may be a check on the other."

YOUR GOVERNMENT: HOW IT WORKS examines some of the major parts of that central authority, the federal government. It explains how various officials, agencies, and departments operate and explores the political organizations that have grown up to serve the needs of government.

Introduction

The federal government as presented in the Constitution was more an idealistic construct than a practical administrative structure. It was barely functional when it came into being.

This was especially true of the executive branch. The Constitution did not describe the executive branch in any detail. After vesting executive power in the president, it assumed the existence of "executive departments" without specifying what these departments should be. Congress began defining their functions in 1789 by creating the Departments of State, Treasury, and War.

President Washington, assisted by Secretary of the Treasury Alexander Hamilton, equipped the infant republic with a working administrative structure. Congress also continued that process by creating more executive departments as they were needed.

Throughout the 19th century, the number of federal government workers increased at a consistently faster rate than did the population. Increasing concerns about the politicization of public service led to efforts—bitterly opposed by politicians—to reform it in the latter part of the century.

The 20th century saw considerable expansion of the federal establishment. More importantly, it saw growing impatience with bureaucracy in society as a whole.

The Great Depression during the 1930s confronted the nation with its greatest crisis since the Civil War. Under Franklin Roosevelt, the New Deal reshaped the federal government, assigning it a variety of new responsibilities and greatly expanding its regulatory functions. By 1940, the number of federal workers passed the 1 million mark.

Critics complained of big government and bureaucracy. Business owners resented federal regulation. Conservatives worried about the impact of paternalistic government on self-reliance, on community responsibility, and on economic and personal freedom.

When the United States entered World War II in 1941, government agencies focused their energies on supporting the war effort. By the end of World War II, federal civilian employment had risen to 3.8 million. With peace, the federal establishment declined to around 2 million in 1950. Then growth resumed, reaching 2.8 million by the 1980s.

A large part of this growth was the result of the national government assuming new functions such as: affirmative action in civil rights, environmental protection, and safety and health in the workplace.

Some critics became convinced that the national government was a steadily growing behemoth swallowing up the liberties of the people. The 1980s brought new intensity to the debate about government growth. Foes of Washington bureaucrats preferred local government, feeling it more responsive to popular needs.

But local government is characteristically the government of the locally powerful. Historically, the locally powerless have often won their human and constitutional rights by appealing to the national government. The national government has defended racial justice against local bigotry, upheld the Bill of Rights against local vigilantism, and protected natural resources from local greed. It has civilized industry and secured the rights of labor organizations. Had the states' rights creed prevailed, perhaps slavery would still exist in the United States.

Americans are still of two minds. When pollsters ask large, spacious questions—Do you think government has become too involved in your lives? Do you think government should stop regulating business?—a sizable majority opposes big government. But when asked specific questions about the practical work of government—Do you favor Social Security? Unemployment compensation? Medicare? Health and safety standards in factories? Environmental protection?—a sizable majority approves of intervention.

We do not like bureaucracy, but we cannot live without it. We need its genius for organizing the intricate details of our daily lives. Without bureaucracy, modern society would collapse. It would be impossible to run any of the large public and private organizations we depend on without bureaucracy's division of labor and hierarchy of authority. The challenge is to keep these necessary structures of our civilization flexible, efficient, and capable of innovation.

More than 200 years after the drafting of the Constitution, Americans still rely on government but also mistrust it. These attitudes continue to serve us well. What we mistrust, we are more likely to monitor. And government needs our constant attention if it is to avoid inefficiency, incompetence, and arbitrariness. Without our informed participation, it cannot serve us individually or help us as a people to attain the lofty goals of the Founding Fathers.

The United States Capitol building in Washington, D.C., where 435 members of the House of Representatives meet for each session of Congress.

CHAPTER **1**

What Is the U.S. House of Representatives?

ARTICLE I, SECTION 1, of the United States **Constitution** set the guidelines for the creation of the Congress of the United States. When the first Congress met in 1789, it was made up of senators and representatives from only 13 states. Today there are 50 states in the Union. These states send 100 senators and 435 representatives to Washington, D.C., for each session of Congress.

Congress is made up of two chambers. The House of Representatives is usually called simply the House and its members are called representatives. The other chamber, or house, of Congress is the Senate. Its members are called senators.

The responsibilities of Congress have grown greatly since 1789. Congress has successfully met the challenges of over 200 years of change. The purpose of Congress, however, is the same as it was when the first session came to order so long ago—making the laws by which the nation lives.

George Washington presides over the Continental Congress in 1787. After debate, it was agreed that the number of representatives each state sends to the House would be based on the state's population.

The Idea of a House of Representatives

In 1787 the Constitutional Convention established the form of national government. Its delegates could not, however, agree on how each state should be represented in Congress. States with large populations wanted representation to be decided by population. The states with smaller populations wanted equal representation for each state. This was a difficult problem for the men who wrote the Constitution. It was finally settled by the Great Compromise.

The 13 original states agreed that representatives would be elected to the House based on the population of each state. The greater the population of a state, the more representatives that state could seat in the House. In the Senate each state was given two senators, regardless of population. This compromise pleased all the states.

How Many People Serve in the House?

The Constitution says Congress has the power to decide how representatives are shared among the states. It says that each member of the House must represent at least 30,000 persons, and each state must have at least one representative. The number of representatives from each state is decided by a **census** taken every 10 years.

The first House had 59 members. But it was formed before the first census had been taken. So by the end of the first Congress, the House had seated 65 representatives from 13 states. Time passed, new states joined the Union, and the nation's population increased. As a result the House grew in numbers. Its membership reached 435 in 1913. In that year Congress passed a law that limited the number of representatives to 435. This was a sensible change to the original system of deciding representation on population only. If that had continued, the House of Representatives would have had over a 1,000 members and the House could not have done its job.

Then, in 1959, Alaska and Hawaii became states, and the House gained two more members. After the 1960 census the House was again limited by law to 435 members. With the most recent estimates of the population of the United States, there is one representative for each 626,720 people.

The District of Columbia, American Samoa, Guam, and the Virgin Islands each send a delegate to the House. Puerto Rico is represented by a resident commissioner. Although these officials do not represent a state in the Union, they do vote in committees and in some cases in the full House.

What Does Congress Do?

The main work of Congress is to make federal laws. The Constitution says that Congress must meet to do this at least once every year—at noon on January 3, unless by law a different day is chosen. A Congress begins in January of the year following the election of its members, lasts two years, and is divided into two, one-year sessions. The House of Representatives agrees on its rules on the opening day of each Congress.

The Senate and House of Representatives have equal functions and powers. Therefore, one is not called the "upper" house; nor is the other called the "lower" house. There are, however, some differences in the two chambers: Only the House of Representatives may introduce bills about finance, taxes, and government spending. Any steps toward impeachment must begin in the House. Only the Senate can discuss and allow international treaties and approve certain nominations made by the president.

In some cases, both chambers of Congress work together. One of these is impeachment. This is the process of bringing a public official to trial for wrongdoing. Congress can impeach the president of the United States and federal judges. Each house of Congress has an exact role to play in this process. The House of Representatives presents the charges against the official to the Senate. The Senate then acts as the jury in the official's trial. The chief justice of the Supreme Court is the judge in an impeachment trial.

Both houses meet together on the sixth day of January following a presidential election (unless by law a different day is chosen). Together they count the electoral votes of the election. If no candidate wins a majority of the total electoral votes, the House of Representatives chooses the president from among the three candidates with the largest number of popular votes. Each state delegation has one vote in this decision.

How Does the House Work?

The House of Representatives is divided among members of mainly two **political parties**—the Democratic and

Members of the House Judiciary Committee meet on October 5, 1998, to recommend that Congress open a formal investigation into the grounds for impeaching President Clinton. The protocol for impeachment is defined in the Constitution.

Republican parties. The party with the most members elected to the House is called the majority party. This party elects the Speaker of the House, the leader who controls all legislative activities.

Most of the work of the House is done by committees made up of members of both parties. Committees have various tasks. Among other things, they select the

House Ways and Means Committee Chairman Bill Archer speaks at a news conference to announce a major tax cut. The Committee is one of the House's 19 standing committees.

agenda and prepare bills for the consideration of the whole House. They also control the operation of the House.

There are 19 standing committees. Each focuses on one area of government policy and has several subcommittees. These committees do more than consider bills for legislation. For example, they also hold hearings on topics of public interest and conduct investigations.

Since the days of the early **republic,** the business of the House of Representatives has greatly increased. Today it is in session almost year-round. It processes many thousands of bills each year and helps enact several hundred public laws. In addition to elected representatives, over 10,000 individuals are employed to accomplish this important work.

Winston Churchill making an election speech in 1908. People in democratic nations, such as Great Britain, choose their leaders by electing them.

CHAPTER **2**

An Orderly House:
The Election and Leadership of the House of Representatives

How the House of Representatives Is Elected

ELECTIONS ARE THE MOST vital political feature of a democratic nation. There are many democratic nations in the world, including the United States, Canada, Japan, Mexico, and Great Britain. Elections are important to these countries because they give people the chance to choose their own leaders. Through elections, a nation can also replace leaders who have become unpopular. This is one of the ways that the power of a government is limited.

An election is a process of choosing one person from among a group of candidates to fill a political position. This is done by voting. The people who vote are called the electorate.

Why Are Elections Held?

Elections are used to select officers at any level of government. In the United States mayors of cities, supervisors of counties, some judges and sheriffs, members of state legislatures, members of Congress, the president and vice president of the United States, and many other officers are elected.

Who Wins or Loses an Election?

Elections may be won in a variety of ways. In many elections the winning candidate must win by a plurality. This means that he or she receives more votes than any other candidate. In other elections a winning candidate must win by a majority. This means that he or she receives more than half the total number of votes cast.

What Makes an Election Really Democratic?

The following are the criteria for a democratic election:

A democratic election provides citizens with many freedoms and safeguards not allowed in nondemocratic countries.

1. Any person who meets the minimum requirements, such as age or citizenship, must be allowed to run for office. In nondemocratic countries candidates may be picked by government officials.
2. People must be able to vote in private. This protects them from being threatened by people who

disagree with their vote. In nondemocratic countries citizens may fear punishment if they vote against the government.

3. Votes must be accurately and fairly counted. In nondemocratic countries votes may be miscounted or even destroyed so that a particular individual will be sure to win.

4. Any person meeting the minimum requirements of age, citizenship, and residence must be allowed to vote. In nondemocratic countries people may be prevented from voting, either by law or intimidation.

The House of Representatives is selected through an electoral process. This is the method used to select candidates, register voters, and manage voting. The ways these things are accomplished vary throughout the United States. The national government establishes all federal election requirements. Each state can establish its own election and voting laws. Many of the states, however, adopt rules and practices like those of the **federal government.** This avoids problems that may come from having two different systems.

There are two major political parties in the United States—the Democratic party and the Republican party. These are groups of voters who share similar political views, or philosophies. There are also numerous smaller political parties. All these parties are an important feature of the American political system. Democrats and Republicans select most of the candidates who run for public office in the United States. They also provide support to candidates in the form of money, advice, and publicity.

To vote in a state or national election, a person must be a U.S. citizen and be 18 years of age. States also require periods of residency before voting is allowed. Before a citizen can vote, he or she must register, or sign up, with election authorities. If a citizen fails to register, he or she will not be allowed to vote. The reason for this requirement is that an individual can vote only once in any election. At the time a person votes, his or her name is checked off the list of registered voters.

The Makeup of the House

To serve in the House of Representatives, a person must be at least 25 years old, a U.S. citizen for at least 7 years, and, at the time of election, a resident of the state in which he or she is chosen. If these requirements are not met, a person cannot legally serve in the House, even if that person is elected. Members of the House of Representatives serve two-year **terms.** The entire House stands for re-election every two years.

The person who leads the House is called the Speaker of the House. The Speaker is chosen by vote of the party to which he or she belongs and must then be elected by a majority vote of the full House. This position is the most powerful of all the House leadership positions. An example of a strong Speaker of the House was Thomas ("Tip") O'Neill who held the job from 1977 to 1986.

The Speaker rules on points of order, recognizes members who wish to speak, and influences the scheduling of legislation and the course of debate. The Speaker also assigns bills to the committees. This task is important because sometimes the committee to which a bill is referred determines the fate of that bill. One committee may approve a bill whereas another may not.

The Speaker of the House also influences the House Rules Committee. This powerful committee decides which bills that have been reported by other committees will actually come to the House floor for a vote. He or she also determines the rules for debating and voting on those bills.

Appointments to the House/Senate conference committees are made by the Speaker. He or she also chairs the majority party committee that assigns members of that

party to committees and nominates heads of committees. The Speaker votes in the House; this vote, however, is traditionally used only to break a tie vote.

Speaker of the House Thomas P. O'Neill occupied this most powerful of all House leadership positions from 1977 to 1986.

The majority leader is the majority party's chief legislative spokesperson. The majority leader develops and coordinates the party's legislative program in cooperation with the Speaker and other party leaders and also works to achieve the party's legislative goals.

The majority whip, together with deputy and assistant whips, is responsible for rounding up votes in support of legislation. When a close vote is expected, the whips count how members are likely to vote.

In the minority party these positions are filled by the minority leader and minority whip.

A party caucus is a group to which all of the representatives of a political party belong. (The Republicans call their **caucus** a conference.) The party caucuses make party rules and strategy, elect party leaders, approve committee assignments, and sometimes adopt party positions on legislation.

Televised proceedings, such as President Clinton's delivery of the State of the Union address to Congress in 1999, are taken care of by the chief administrative officer of the House.

For example, House Republicans have a Committee on Research, which serves as the research arm of the Republican Conference; a Policy Committee, which examines and advises House Republicans on major pending legislation; and a Committee on Committees, which assigns Republicans to committees.

House Democrats have the Democratic Steering and Policy Committee, which does similar work as the Republican committees.

Other officers are elected by the House of Representatives. One of these is the chaplain. Every session of the House opens with a prayer offered by the House chaplain or a guest chaplain. The other officers are the clerk, the sergeant at arms, the chief administrative officer, and the parliamentarian.

The clerk keeps the seal of the House (which is used to stamp all bills) and administers the main legislative activities of the House. Among other things, the clerk calls the members to order at the beginning of the first session of each Congress, takes all votes, certifies the passage of bills, processes all legislation, and distributes documents.

The sergeant at arms maintains the order of the House under the direction of the Speaker. As a member of the U.S. Capitol Police Board, the sergeant at arms is the chief law enforcement officer for the House. The sergeant at arms enforces the rules relating to the privileges of the Hall of the House, including admission to the galleries.

The chief administrative officer takes care of other House support services, including the payroll, the benefits, the postal operations and internal mail distribution, the office furnishings, and the televised proceedings.

The parliamentarian of the House assists the Speaker or the chairperson in ruling on questions about the proper order and rules of debate.

President Bill Clinton (left) and Education Secretary Richard Riley (right) on their way to speak at a White House event. Secretary Riley, as a member of the presidents's cabinet, can propose a law to the House of Representatives under the right of executive communication.

CHAPTER 3

What Is a Bill and Where Does It Come From?

Where Laws Get Started

IDEAS FOR THE LEGISLATION considered in the House of Representatives come from many sources—often from a member of the House itself. Sometimes a candidate for a seat in the House will center his or her campaign on a special issue of public interest. A candidate often promises to introduce legislation on that issue, if elected. After being elected to the House, a member may become aware of needed **amendments** to an existing law or learn of a law that should be repealed. Or the member may propose an entirely new bill.

Individual citizens may have very good ideas for laws. Citizen groups and associations often want old laws changed or new laws passed. Every citizen of the United States, therefore, has the right to petition Congress—that is, they can try to convince a member of the

House to introduce a bill in Congress. The right to petition Congress is guaranteed by the First Amendment to the Constitution. It says:

> Congress shall make no law respecting an establishment of religion, or prohibiting the free exercise thereof; or abridging the freedom of speech, or of the press; or the right of the people peaceably to assemble, and to petition the government for a redress of grievances.

Many organizations and individuals pay careful attention to laws that concern their interests. Their knowledge is usually not available to a member of the House.

Any one of the 50 state legislatures can also suggest a bill to Congress. To do this, they must pass a resolution called a memorial. Memorials are requests from a state that the U.S. Congress enact certain federal laws. A representative introduces the state legislature's proposal to the House.

Another source of ideas for laws is the executive communication. This comes from the president of the United States, a member of the president's cabinet, or the head of a federal agency. An executive communication is a letter to the Speaker of the House of Representatives. Included with this letter is a draft of a proposed bill. The Speaker sends this to the right committee or committees. There the communication may be revised before being introduced to the full House.

One example of an executive communication is the president's budget proposal. This is the basis of the **appropriation** bills that are drafted by the House Committee on Appropriations.

Anyone may draft a bill, but only a member of Congress can introduce legislation. The person who does this is called the sponsor of that bill. A bill is officially in the legislative process after it is numbered, referred to a committee, and printed by the Government Printing Office.

Pork carcasses lined up for inspection in a turn-of-the-century Chicago packinghouse. President Theodore Roosevelt (pictured below), working with a cooperative Congress, enacted the Pure Food and Drug Act and a Meat Inspection act.

How to Tell a Bill from a Resolution

Proposals for laws are made in one of four ways: a bill, a joint resolution, a concurrent resolution, and a simple resolution. How many of these are usually introduced in Congress? During the first year of the 104th Congress (1995–1996), for example, 6,545 bills and 263 joint resolutions were introduced in the House and Senate. Of this number, 4,344 bills and 198 joint resolutions began in the House of Representatives.

The bill is the form used for most legislation and can start in the House of Representatives or the Senate. There is one exception. Article I, Section 7, of the Constitution says:

> All bills for raising Revenue shall originate in the House of Representatives; but the Senate may propose or concur with Amendments as on other Bills.

This means that only the House can introduce bills about taxation. Traditionally, general appropriation bills also begin in the House.

There are two types of bills—public and private. A public bill concerns the general public of the United States. A private bill affects only an individual citizen or a private entity like a corporation. A private bill is used in matters such as immigration and in claims against the United States.

A bill must be agreed to in identical form by both the House and Senate, and it must receive presidential approval. If it clears these hurdles, it becomes the law of the land. If the president does not favor the bill, the president may **veto** the bill within 10 days. In this case the presidential veto can be overridden by a two-thirds vote in each chamber of Congress.

If the president does not return a bill to Congress within 10 days while Congress is in session, the bill is automatically enacted and becomes a law. If the session of Congress ends before the president can return a bill with objections, it cannot become law without the president's signature. This is known as a pocket veto.

The text of a bill always begins with the following words:

> *Be it enacted by the Senate and House of Representatives of the United States of America in Congress assembled . . . .*

This clause is called the enacting clause. It was defined by law in 1871. All bills begin with the enacting clause, whether they come from the House or from the Senate.

President Lyndon B. Johnson signs the Tonkin Resolution in 1964. This resolution gave him power to take any necessary action, without prior Congressional approval, to protect American troops in Vietnam.

Joint resolutions begin in the House of Representatives *or* the Senate, not from both houses at the same time, as the name seems to imply. The House and Senate do, however, work together, first one and then the other, to pass a resolution or a bill.

A bill and a joint resolution are very much alike. One difference is that a joint resolution may include a preamble, which describes why the resolution is necessary. This preamble comes before the resolving clause—a statement similar to the enacting clause. This too was created by law in 1871. It is the same for all joint resolutions and reads as follows:

> *Resolved by the Senate and House of Representatives of the United States of America in Congress assembled . . . .*

Joint resolutions become law in the same way as bills do. The exception to this is a resolution made to amend the Constitution. Such a joint resolution must be approved by a vote of two-thirds of both houses of Congress. It is not presented to the president for approval, instead it is sent to all 50 states. Each state legislature votes to approve or disapprove the resolution. Three-fourths of the states must approve the resolution within the time period specified in the joint resolution. If this occurs, the amendment becomes part of the Constitution.

Concurrent resolutions affect the operations of both houses of Congress. Concurrent and simple resolutions do not concern federal laws. They are, therefore, not presented to the president for approval. They deal with the facts, principles, opinions, and purposes of the two Houses. A concurrent resolution is not the same as a bill. When a concurrent resolution is approved by both houses, it is signed by the clerk of the House and the secretary of the Senate and then published in the Statutes at Large volume covering that session of Congress.

Simple resolutions concern the rules, the operation, or the opinion of either the House or the Senate, not both. They are considered only by the chamber in which they are introduced. When approved, a simple resolution is validated by the clerk of the House of Representatives or the secretary of the Senate and is published in the ***Congressional Record.***

RJR Nabisco chairman and CEO Steven Goldstone (center) testifies about the tobacco industry before the House Commerce Committee. Tobacco industry leaders had submitted a bill to Congress requesting immunity from future lawsuits.

CHAPTER 4

The Journey from Bill to Law

Introduction

FOR A BILL TO become a law it must first be introduced in Congress. A representative, the resident commissioner from Puerto Rico, or the delegates in the House of Representatives can introduce a bill any time the House is in session. This procedure is very simple; permission is not necessary and blank forms for an original bill are always available. A bill is introduced by a member placing it in a wooden box, called "the hopper," located on the side of the rostrum in the House chamber.

Each bill has a sponsor—the member introducing the bill—and may have an unlimited number of cosponsors. The sponsor's signature must appear on the bill before it is accepted for introduction. The House does not publicly read bills or their titles when they are introduced. Instead the title is printed in the *Congressional Record*. Finally, the bill is assigned its own number.

Referral to Committee

The Speaker of the House then refers the bill to the correct committees. The bill is sent to the Government Printing Office, printed, and copies are sent to the document rooms of both houses of Congress. There the bill is available to members of Congress. The general public also has access to the printed and electronic versions of the bill.

When the chairperson of the committee to which the bill was referred receives copies, the clerk of the committee enters it on the committee's legislative calendar.

Committee Action

Committee action is the most important part of the legislative process. A bill is carefully considered in the committee and the public is given the opportunity to comment on its content and value. A bill can be referred to a subcommittee or considered by the committee as a whole. The amount of work accomplished during this phase in the process of legislation is not often appreciated by the pub-

President Harry S. Truman (center) addresses a joint session of Congress in the House Chamber. "The hopper" (circled in photo), where House members place bills they are introducing, is the box attached to the side of the rostrum to the President's right.

lic. This work includes agency reports or public hearings, business meetings or markup, and committee action to report a bill.

Agency Reports

One of the first things a committee does when it receives a bill is to send copies to interested departments and agencies of the government. These agencies return reports to the committee. These reports supply information to the committee and are seriously considered.

Public Hearings

The committee or subcommittee often schedules public hearings on the bill. A public announcement of the date, place, and subject of this hearing must be made at least one week (or at the earliest possible date) before the hearing begins. Personal notice of the hearing is sometimes sent to individuals, organizations, and government departments and agencies that have a special interest in a certain bill. They may have useful information for the committee.

Hearings are the committee's opportunity to hear the views of the executive branch, other public officials, experts, supporters, and opponents of the legislation. Cabinet officers and high-ranking civil and military officials of the government, as well as interested private individuals, testify in public hearings.

In most cases these hearings are required to be open to the public. Sometimes sensitive testimony, evidence, or other matters are considered in a committee hearing. For example, this information may endanger national security, reveal law enforcement information, or violate a law or a rule of the House. In such a case the committee can vote to close the hearing.

A transcript of the public hearing is made available in the office of the clerk of the committee. Sometimes the complete transcript is printed and distributed by the committee.

Representative Patsy Mink of Hawaii speaks at a hearing of the House Education and the Workforce Committee about the 1996 Teamsters elections.

Business Meetings or Markup

After hearings are complete, a subcommittee considers the bill in a session known as the markup session. Here the members mark up the bill—that is, they make changes and amendments before sending it back to the full committee. If a subcommittee votes not to report legislation to the full committee, the bill dies.

In a markup session the opinions of the minority and majority are studied in detail. Then a vote is taken to decide to report the bill favorably, unfavorably, or without recommendation to the full committee. The subcommittee can also suggest that the committee table the bill. To table a bill means to postpone action indefinitely on it.

Committee Action to Report a Bill

The various subcommittees report on bills at full committee meetings. At this time bills are read for amendment. Any member can offer relevant amendments. These amendments are only proposals to change the bill. They must be accepted or rejected by the House itself.

The full committee then votes on its recommendation to the House. This is called "ordering a bill reported." The committee has a choice: to report the bill favorably or to table the bill. If the committee votes to report the bill favorably to the House, it may report the bill in one of three ways: with amendments, without amendments, or as a clean bill. In a clean bill, the committee rewrites the bill to incorporate all amendments.

This new bill is introduced in the House by the chairperson of the committee. It is then referred back to the committee, which reports it favorably to the House.

Finally, a committee may table a bill. This means that it does not take action on it. This prevents further action on that bill.

Publication of a Written Report

When a committee votes to report a bill favorably to the House, it writes a committee report. This report describes the purpose of the bill. It gives the House the reasons why the committee wants it approved and explains each section of the bill. If the bill changes any existing law, the text of the changed law is included in the report. Also included in a committee's report are the amendments made by the committee and the executive branch's opinion of the bill.

At the time a committee approves a bill, a member of the committee can file minority, or dissenting, views about the legislation. These are included in the report on the bill. Committee reports are filed while the House is in session. At that time the report is assigned a number and is sent to the Government Printing Office for printing.

Committee reports are very useful. They give the legislative history of a law. This information about the purpose and meaning of the law is used by courts, executive departments, and the public.

Scheduling Action in the House

After a bill is reported back to the House, it is placed in chronological order on a calendar. The House has several different legislative calendars. The Speaker and the majority leader usually decide when and in what order bills appear on the calendar.

The House of Representatives has five calendars of business: the Union Calendar, the House Calendar, the Private Calendar, the Corrections Calendar, and the Calendar of Motions to Discharge Committees. These calendars are published each day the House is in session.

When a public bill is favorably reported to the House, it is assigned a calendar number on the Union Calendar or the House Calendar. These are the two main calendars of business.

The main calendar is called the Union Calendar. Here is how the rules of the House describe this calendar:

> A Calendar of the Committee of the Whole House on the state of the Union, to which shall be referred bills raising revenue, general appropriation bills, and bills of a public character directly or indirectly appropriating money or property.

Most public bills and resolutions reported to the House are placed on the Union Calendar.

The rules also call for another calendar—the House Calendar. All public bills which do not have to do with money or property are found on this calendar. For example, a member may introduce a bill to honor a citizen for a special accomplishment. This would cost no money and has nothing to do with federal property. This public bill would, therefore, be placed on the House Calendar, not on the Union Calendar.

Private bills that are reported to the House are placed on a third calendar, called the Private Calendar. On the first and third Tuesdays of each month, bills on the Private Calendar are considered.

The House often improves and corrects the many federal rules, regulations, and court decisions. These may include rules about who can use federal property, how a person must apply for citizenship, and so on. This work is scheduled on the Corrections Calendar. On the second and fourth Tuesdays of each month, the clerk calls any bill that has been on the Corrections Calendar for three legislative days. A three-fifths vote of the members is required to pass a bill from the Corrections Calendar. If a bill is rejected, it can be brought up for consideration, just as any other bill, on the House or Union Calendar.

The House uses one more calendar to schedule its business. This is the Calendar of Motions to Discharge Committees. A majority of the members of the House may decide to bring a bill out of the control of a committee. They may do this, for example, in order to guarantee that the bill would be debated by the whole House. To do this they must sign a motion to discharge the committee from considering a public bill or resolution. This motion is placed on the Calendar of Motions to Discharge Committees.

Some bills and resolutions are more important than others. If the order of the calendars was used to decide the order bills would be called before the House, some vital legislation would be delayed. A good illustration of this is the president's proposal for the federal budget. Unless this proposal is debated and passed by Congress, the government has no money to spend. The proposal must be considered immediately after it is reported. The House, therefore, has a system to accommodate the most important bills.

If all the members in the House chamber agree to consider a bill, it is called unanimous consent. Such an agreement usually occurs only when the Speaker is sure that the majority and minority leaderships have no objection to the bill.

Bills can be considered by the House out of their order on the calendar if the Committee on Rules issues a special resolution or "rule." The Committee on Rules always decides the order of business in the House. The chairperson of a committee that has reported a bill may want to change the date for its consideration by the whole House. He or she may do this to be sure that certain members are present for the debate. Therefore the chairperson asks the Committee on Rules for a resolution that will change the date for the bill's consideration.

Representatives can also file a motion to stop the Committee on Rules from passing a rule for the consideration of a public bill. On the second and fourth Mondays of each month, such a motion is debated. If it passes, the House immediately considers this resolution. If it is adopted, the House enacts it.

Also, a representative is allowed to present a motion in writing to bring a bill out of the control of a committee. Such a motion is called a motion to discharge committee and can happen only after the bill has been in the committee for 30 days. This would be done, for example, if the committee is sure to reject the bill and the member wants it to be debated by the whole House.

If the motion to discharge is passed, the House can immediately consider the bill under the general rules of the House. If the House votes against the motion, the bill is returned to its proper calendar.

Another way to consider a bill out of its calendar order is called a motion to suspend the rules. Only the Speaker of the House considers this motion. If approved, the Speaker can then pass a public bill or resolution. This can happen on Monday and Tuesday of each week or during the last six days of a session of Congress. This motion is used only for public measures that are not controversial. The rules may only be suspended when a quorum (or 218 members) is present. (A quorum is the minimum number of members required to be present before the House can carry on business.)

On Wednesday of each week the standing committees, in alphabetical order, can call up for consideration any bill it has already reported. This is called calendar Wednesday. A vote of a simple majority of the members passes the measure. Calendar Wednesday provides a way for the House to consider a bill when the Committee on Rules has not reported a rule for that bill.

The House of Representatives governs the District of Columbia, which is the federal zone in which the nation's capital city, Washington, is located. The Committee on Government Reform and Oversight calls for consideration of District of Columbia business, such as money matters, civil statutes, or criminal law. This business is considered on the second and fourth Mondays of each month.

Certain things handled by the House are called privileged matters—that is, they are not controlled by any other rules of the House. Conference reports, veto messages from the president, and some amendments to measures by the Senate are examples of privileged matters. Certain reports from House committees are also privileged.

Privileged matters are allowed to interrupt the normal order of House business. A representative can call up such a matter at almost any time. It is then considered immediately. This is usually done with the knowledge of the majority and minority floor leaders so that the members of both parties have advance notice of the interruption.

Legislation is always considered (debated) by the entire membership of the House of Representatives. Time is given for the debate of new bills and for adding amendments to them.

To speed up this process and to consider general appropriation bills—bills that are used to raise or spend money for the federal government—a member can move that the House act as the Committee of the Whole House on the State of the Union (also called the Committee of the Whole). The representatives present in the chamber vote to temporarily become the Committee of the Whole. As such, they can work with a quorum of less than the 218 quorum required in the House. A quorum in the Committee of the Whole is only 100 members. All measures on the Union Calendar must be considered in the Committee of the Whole.

When the House acts as the Committee of the Whole, the Speaker leaves the chair after appointing a chairperson to preside. All the representatives present are automatically members of the Committee of the Whole.

Debate is controlled by rules adopted at the opening of each Congress. The House also uses *Jefferson's Manual,* prepared by Thomas Jefferson for his own guidance as president of the Senate from 1797 to 1801. In addition, it uses various books of parliamentary patterns dating from the earliest days of Congress.

Portrait of Thomas Jefferson. House debate today is still controlled using Jefferson's Manual, *which contains rules drawn up by Jefferson when he was president of the Senate.*

The Committee of the Whole begins work on a bill with general debate. During this time an accurate count is kept of the time used for debate by both parties. The chairperson ends the debate when all the time allowed has been used. Then the second reading, a section-by-section reading of the bill, begins.

During this time, amendments can be suggested as a section is read. The amendments are then debated under special rules.

A House rule known as the *germaneness rule,* does not allow amendments that are different from the subject of the bill being debated. This rule is one of the most important rules of the House of Representatives. A group the size of the House must remain focused on a particular subject. Germaneness (relevance) means that all suggested amendments must directly relate to the bill being debated.

When the second reading has been completed, the committee is finished considering a bill for amendment. Next, the committee "rises"—that is, the committee reports the bill to the House, with the amendments that have been adopted. When it rises, the Committee of the Whole reverts to its status as the House of Representatives. The chairperson of the committee is replaced by the Speaker of the House, and the House then acts on the bill.

House Action

Debate on a bill is ended by a motion that "orders the previous question." This motion must be approved by a majority of the members, with a quorum present. It can also be passed by a special rule that orders the previous question when the Committee of the Whole rises. The Speaker then asks, "Shall the bill be engrossed and read a third time?" If the members agree to this question, the title of the bill is read and a vote is taken.

There can be two types of vote at this time. If the previous question has been ordered by the rising of the

Committee of the Whole, the House votes on the amendments reported by the committee. Or, unless a motion to recommit is offered, the House immediately votes on the passage of the bill with the amendments it has adopted.

After the previous question has been ordered, the Speaker calls on a member of the minority party who is opposed to the bill. This member can offer a motion to recommit (return) the bill to a committee. The motion to recommit normally contains amendments to change the bill before it is passed.

After the House passes or rejects a bill, a motion to reconsider it is automatically made. This is done because the vote of the House on a bill is not final until there has been an opportunity to reconsider it.

Voting

Voting in the Committee of the Whole or in the House is by voice vote, by division vote, or by recorded vote. (The House also uses a fourth way, the yea-and-nay vote, discussed later.)

For the first vote, a voice vote, the chair asks, "As many as are in favor say 'aye.' As many as are opposed, say 'no'." The Chair decides the result by comparing the loudness of the ayes and noes.

If the result of a voice vote is hard to determine, a member or the chair may demand a division vote. To conduct a division vote, the chair says, "As many as are in favor will rise and stand until counted." After counting those in favor, the chair calls on those opposed to stand and be counted.

A member can also request a recorded vote. This request must be supported by at least one-fifth of a quorum of the House, or 25 members in the Committee of the Whole. This vote is taken electronically. After the recorded vote, the names of those voting and those not voting are entered in the record.

YEA 41   NAY 58

Motion to Open
the Debate

Electronic vote tally on the Senate floor, showing the defeat of a motion to call witnesses in President Clinton's impeachment trial.

In the electronic voting system, vote stations are attached to certain chairs in the chamber. Each vote station has a vote card slot and four buttons, marked "yea," "nay," "present," and "open." These buttons are lit when a vote is in progress and the system is ready to accept votes. Each member has a personalized vote-ID card. Members vote by putting their card into a vote station and pressing a button to indicate their choice.

In the House, if the yeas and nays are demanded, the Speaker asks those in favor of taking the vote by this method to stand and be counted. One-fifth of the members present must vote in favor of the yeas and nays. When the yeas and nays are ordered, the Speaker says, "As many as are in favor of the proposition will vote 'aye.' As many as are opposed will vote 'no'." The clerk records these votes on the electronic system or calls the roll and reports the result to the Speaker.

The rules of the House say that three-fifths of the members must vote in favor of a bill, a joint resolution, or an amendment for it to pass.

Engrossment and Referral to the Senate

The final copy of a bill is called the engrossed bill. The preparation of a final copy of a bill is very complicated. Some bills have many amendments, and these are sometimes very detailed. It is not unusual to have more than 100 amendments on a single bill. Each amendment must be put in the proper place in the bill, exactly as it was written. The spelling and punctuation must be just as it was adopted by the House. The Senate must receive a copy of the bill in the very form in which it passed in the House. The preparation of this engrossed copy is the job of the enrolling clerk, who works under the clerk of the House.

The enrolling clerk is given the official clerk's copy of the bill as it was reported by the standing committee, along with each amendment adopted by the House. Using this material, the enrolling clerk prepares the engrossed copy of the bill as passed. When this is done, the measure is officially called an act. This means that it is the action of one body of the Congress. The act is printed on blue paper and is signed by the clerk of the House.

Next the act is sent to the Senate. There it follows a similar path through committee and Senate action. The Senate may approve the bill as received, reject it, ignore it, or change it.

Return from the Senate

The Senate often returns bills to the House with new amendments. The Speaker may want to send the Senate amendments to a committee for consideration. If the amendments are minor, however, any member can ask for unanimous consent to agree to the Senate amendments. If there is no objection, the amendments are declared to be agreed to. The bill is then ready to be enrolled for presentation to the president of the United States. Most Senate amendments, however, must be considered and approved in the Committee of the Whole.

Conference Committee Action

If the Senate makes only minor changes to a bill, it usually goes directly back to the House for acceptance. If the Senate makes major changes to the bill, however, a conference committee is formed. The conference committee is sometimes called the "third house of congress." It is made up of members, who are called "managers," of both chambers of Congress. The conference committee works to harmonize the differences between the House and Senate versions of the bill.

If the conference committee can't agree, the legislation dies. If the committee can reach an agreement, it submits a conference report. This report describes the committee's recommendations for changes to the bill. Both the House and the Senate must approve the conference report.

Enrollment

When the bill has been agreed to in identical form by both the House and Senate, a copy of the bill is enrolled for presentation to the president.

Careful preparation of the enrolled bill is an important task. It must show every amendment agreed to by the House and Senate. To do this, the enrolling clerk of the House uses the original engrossed bill, the engrossed Senate amendments, the signed conference report, any messages from the Senate, and notes of the final action by the House.

Sometimes as many as 500 amendments have been added to a bill. Each of these must be in the enrollment exactly as they were agreed upon.

House Speaker Newt Gingrich (seated, left) and Senate Majority Leader Trent Lott (seated, right) sign an enrolled bill on IRS reform in July 1998. After Vice President Al Gore signed it, the bill was given to President Clinton for signature.

The enrolled bill is printed on parchment paper and certified by the clerk of the House. It is examined for accuracy by the Committee on House Oversight. Then it goes to the Speaker of the House for signature. Next the vice president of the United States signs it. (The vice president serves as the president of the Senate.) Finally it is presented to the president.

Presidential Action

If the president approves the bill, he signs it and usually writes the word "approved" and the date. A bill can, however, become law without the president's signature. If the president does not return a bill with his objections within 10 days, it becomes law. However, if Congress adjourns before the 10 days pass, the bill does not become law. This is known as a pocket veto.

If the president vetoes (does not approve) the bill, he returns it to the House with his objections. The House then reconsiders the bill. Under the Constitution, a vote by the yeas and nays is required to pass a bill over the president's veto. If fewer than two-thirds of the members present vote in favor, the bill dies. However, if two-thirds of the members vote in favor, the bill is sent with the president's objections to the Senate.

Two-thirds of the members of the Senate must also vote in favor to pass the bill over the president's veto. If two-thirds of the members of both the Senate and the House vote in favor of passing the bill, the measure becomes the law of the land even though the president objects. It is ready for publication as a binding statute.

In December 1998, the House Committee on the Judiciary took on the special task of organizing a hearing on the possible impeachment of President Clinton.

CHAPTER **5**

The Committees of the House

MANY BILLS AND RESOLUTIONS are introduced each year in the House of Representatives. Few, however, become law. For example, the 106th Congress (1998–1999) introduced 4,874 bills in the House and 2,655 in the Senate. The 105th Congress (1997–1998), introduced 13,882 pieces of legislation. Of these, only 354 became law. This means that 2.6 percent of all the legislation introduced in Congress became law.

What happened to the other 97.4 percent of proposed legislation? Some bills were rejected in votes of the full House or Senate. Others were vetoed by the president. Most of this legislation, however, died in congressional committees, which indicates that the purpose of the congressional committee system is to make sure that only effective and necessary laws are enacted.

What Do Committees Do?

Before a bill can be debated by the full membership of the House or Senate, it must be considered and approved by a committee. A proposed bill is sent to one or more committees, depending on its subject and content. For example, a bill assigning federal funds for agriculture might be sent to three committees: agriculture, appropriations, and budget. The Speaker of the House decides which committees will consider which bill.

If a bill is introduced in the House that deals in any way with federal money, it must first be considered by the House Ways and Means Committee. This committee is probably the busiest in the federal government. Almost two-thirds of the annual federal budget requires the approval of the House Ways and Means Committee.

Committees also do other things besides consider legislation. Some committees take on special tasks; for example, in late 1998 the Committee on the Judiciary organized a presidential impeachment hearing.

There are 19 standing House committees and 16 standing Senate committees. Four joint committees (that are made up of members from both the House and the Senate) provide general oversight of Congress. The House and the Senate can also appoint special select committees to consider specific issues.

Each of the standing committees in the House of Representatives is responsible for certain subjects. All bills affecting a particular area of the law are referred to the committee with authority in that area. For example, the House Committee on the Judiciary considers bills relating to judicial proceedings—for example, the federal courts. It also covers 17 other categories, including constitutional amendments, immigration and naturalization, bankruptcy, patents, copyrights, and trademarks. Over 200 different types of bills are required to be referred to committees.

The Speaker of the House may send a bill to several committees to consider the parts of the bill that concern each committee. The Speaker can also limit the time the committees spend considering bills.

Committee Members

All committees have members from both the Democratic and Republican parties, but the distribution is almost never equal. The majority party decides how many minority members and how many majority members will join a committee. In 1999, for example, the Ways and Means Committee was made up of 23 Republicans and 16 Democrats. There were more Republicans because it was the majority party in the 106th Congress. An exception to this distribution occurs in the Committee on Standards of Official Conduct, in which half of the members are from the majority party and half from the minority party.

At the beginning of each Congress, party caucuses nominate members to be elected to each standing committee. In most cases members of the House may serve on only two committees and four subcommittees. Members usually seek to serve on a committee that covers a field of interest in which they are most qualified. The Committee on the Judiciary, for example, is composed almost entirely of lawyers. Many representatives are experts in the specialty of their particular committee or subcommittee.

Members have **seniority** in a committee according to the order in which they were appointed to the full committee. The ranking majority member with the most continuous service is usually elected chairperson because he or she has the most seniority. No one can serve as chairperson of the same standing committee or subcommittee for more than three Congressional sessions in a row.

Each committee is provided with a professional staff. These people assist the members in the administrative details and problems involved in the committee's operation.

Committee Meetings

Standing committees must schedule meetings at least once a month. The chairperson of the committee may call additional meetings. Three or more members of a standing committee may also request that the chairperson call a special meeting. A majority of the members of the committee may call a special meeting.

In their meetings, committees do more than work on legislation. Each standing committee must continuously review and study the ways laws are applied and administered because the laws and programs created by Congress must be carried out exactly according to the plan passed by Congress.

Reviews help decide if programs and laws should be continued, changed, or ended. Committees also review and study laws to determine if new or additional legislation should be proposed.

Committees of the United States House of Representatives

There are 20 full House committees—19 standing committees and the Permanent Select Committee on Intelligence. The following is a list of the standing committees of the House of Representatives. With each name is a list of the main areas that the committee covers. These lists are not complete, but they do give the reader an idea of the areas of each committee's responsibility.

Committee on Agriculture   All aspects of agriculture and the agricultural industry in general, including protection of birds and animals in forest reserves and activities of the Department of Agriculture.

Committee on Appropriations   Raising of revenue for the support of the government; general responsibility over the organization and operation of executive departments and other executive agencies.

Committee on Banking and Financial Services   Banks and banking; financial aid to commerce and industry; international finance; money and credit, including currency and the issuance of notes and coins.

Committee on the Budget   All resolutions on the budget and other measures concerning levels of budget totals for the government.

Committee on Commerce   Consumer affairs and consumer protection; health and health facilities; interstate and foreign commerce; energy resources; the Department of Energy and the Federal Energy Regulatory Commission.

Committee on Economic and Educational Opportunities   Child labor; convict labor and the entry of goods

The Committee on Banking and Financial Services oversees the printing of currency, such as these newly redesigned $100 bills awaiting shipment to banks all over the country.

made by convicts into interstate commerce; food programs for children in schools; labor standards and statistics; education and labor generally.

Committee on Government Reform and Oversight   The federal civil service; officers and employees of the United States; affairs of the District of Columbia; budget and accounting; holidays and celebrations; the census; postal service; public information and records.

Committee on House Oversight   Committee salaries and expenses of the House; employment of persons by the House; the Library of Congress, the House library, the Smithsonian Institution, and the U.S. National Arboretum; printing and correction of the *Congressional Record;* federal elections generally.

Permanent Select Committee on Intelligence   The Central Intelligence Agency and the national foreign

The Mall in Washington, D.C., with the Washington Monument in the far background. The Committee on Government Reform and Oversight is responsible for the affairs of the District of Columbia.

intelligence program; intelligence-related activities of all other departments and agencies of the government.

Committee on International Relations   Relations of the United States with foreign nations; export controls, including nonproliferation of nuclear technology and nuclear hardware; foreign loans; international commodity agreements; declarations of war; the diplomatic service.

Committee on the Judiciary   Judiciary and judicial proceedings; apportionment of representatives; bankruptcy, mutiny, espionage, and counterfeiting; civil liberties; constitutional amendments; federal courts and judges; immigration and naturalization; national penitentiaries; the Patent Office.

Committee on National Security   Ammunition depots; forts; arsenals; Army, Navy, and Air Force establishments; the Department of Defense; Merchant Marine Academy; military applications of nuclear energy; scientific research and development in support of the armed services; selective service.

Committee on Resources   Fisheries and wildlife; forest reserves and national parks; Geological Survey; international fishing agreements; irrigation and reclamation; military parks, battlefields, and national cemeteries; mineral land laws; mineral resources of the public lands; mining interests generally.

Committee on Rules   The rules, joint rules, and order of business of the House; recesses and final adjournments of Congress; oversight responsibility with respect to the congressional budget process.

Committee on Science   Energy, civil aviation, and environmental research and development; marine research; National Institute of Standards and Technology; weights and measures; NASA; National Space

Apollo II *Astronaut Edwin Aldrin plants the United States flag on the lunar surface. The House Committee on Science oversees NASA activities.*

Council; National Science Foundation; National Weather Service; outer space.

Committee on Small Business   Assistance to and protection of small business, including financial aid, regulatory flexibility, and paperwork reduction; participation of small business enterprises in federal procurement and government contracts.

Committee on Standards of Official Conduct   Measures relating to the code of official conduct.

Committee on Transportation and Infrastructure   Coast Guard; emergencies and natural disasters; flood control and improvement of rivers and harbors; inland waterways; Capitol building and the Senate and House office buildings; construction or maintenance of roads and post roads.

Committee on Veterans' Affairs   Cemeteries of the United States in which veterans are buried; compensation, rehabilitation, and education of veterans; life insurance for service in the armed forces; pensions; veterans civil relief; veterans' hospitals, veterans' medical care, and treatment for veterans.

Committee on Ways and Means   Customs, collection districts, and ports of entry and delivery; reciprocal trade agreements; revenue measures generally; the bonded debt of the United States; tax exempt foundations and charitable trusts; national social security.

Conclusion: The House Represents the People

In 1863—nearly 140 years ago—President Abraham Lincoln was in Gettysburg, Pennsylvania, to help dedicate the national cemetery there. In his speech Lincoln said that he hoped that the government of the United States—"a government, of the people, by the people, and for the people"—would not end after the American Civil War.

Lincoln's simple words describe our government—a government that belongs to the citizens of the country; a government whose purpose is to do what the majority of citizens want it to do. The United States House of Representatives is one very important way that we fulfill this goal.

The people who are elected to the House from your state are *your* representatives in the federal government. They are servants to work for you and for the good of your state and the nation. They work very hard to make our laws and to ensure that these laws are carried out.

How can you participate in your government? Here are three suggestions: (1) Write to your representatives. Thank them for their work. Tell them what you would like see

The Lincoln Memorial honors Abraham Lincoln for preserving a government "of the people, by the people, and for the people." The House of Representatives directly links the will of the people to the federal government.

done in the country. (2) When you are old enough, take part in government by voting in every election. (3) Run for office yourself. These are ways your voice is heard in this government of the people.

Glossary

Amendment—A change or addition to the U.S. Constitution or to a bill in Congress.

Appropriation—The setting aside of money for a specific use.

Census—A governmental count of population. In the United States a census is taken every 10 years.

Caucus—A group to which all representatives of a political party belong and that selects candidates and decides policies.

Congressional Record—A daily publication of the complete proceedings of Congress.

Constitution—The plan of the United States government; the rules of the country.

Federal government—A type of government in which some of the power is at the national level and some of the power is at the state level; also, the central government of the United States.

Political party—A group of people who have similar ideas about how a country should be run.

Republic—A form of government in which there is an elected president rather than a king.

Seniority—A privileged position given according to the length of time a person has continuously served in an organization such as the House of Representatives.

Term—The time for which something lasts; such as the length a person serves in public office.

Veto—The power of the president of the United States to prevent the enactment of measures passed by the legislature.

Further Reading

The Declaration of Independence and the Constitution of the United States. Introduction by Pauline Maier. New York: Bantam Classic, 1998.

Duval, Jill. *Congressional Committees.* New York: Franklin Watts, 1997.

Galloway, George B. *The History of the House of Representatives.* New York: Harper, 1976.

Green, Carol. *Congress.* Chicago: Children's Press, 1985.

Johnson, Charles W. *How Our Laws Are Made.* Washington, D.C.: U.S. Government Printing Office, 1999.

Jones, Veda Boyd. *Government & Politics.* Philadelphia: Chelsea House, 1999.

Maestro, Betsy. *A More Perfect Union: The Story of Our Constitution.* New York: Lothrop, Lee & Shepard Books, 1987.

Maestro, Betsy. *The Voice of the People.* New York: Lothrop, Lee & Shepard Books, 1996.

Weber, Michael. *Our Congress.* Brookfield, CT: Millbrook Press, 1996.

Websites

The Constitution of the United States
http://www.house.gov/Constitution/Constitution.html

The Rules of the 106th Congress (House of Representatives)
http://www.in-search-of.org/106/rules/section3.shtml

U.S. House of Representatives
http://www.house.gov/

Congressional Committees and Subcommittees
Contacting the Congress — **http://www.visi.com/juan/congress/committees.html**

U.S. House of Representatives Committee Office Web Services
http://www.house.gov/house/CommitteeWWW.html

Search the committee web sites
http://www.house.gov/house/CommitteeWWW.html#comsrch

U.S. Legislative Information
Thomas **http://thomas.loc.gov/home/thomas.html?68,15**

Index

ABOUT THE AUTHOR: Daniel Partner is an author who lives and works in northern Vermont. His recent books include *The One Year Book of Poetry* and *Women of Sacred Song: Meditations on Hymns by Women.* He has also written the title *Smoke Screen: Psychological Disorders Related to Nicotine Use* in the Chelsea House series ENCYCLOPEDIA OF PSYCHOLOGICAL DISORDERS.

SENIOR CONSULTING EDITOR Arthur M. Schlesinger, jr. is the leading American historian of our time. He won the Pulitzer Prize for his book *The Age of Jackson* (1945) and again for *A Thousand Days* (1965). This chronicle of the Kennedy Administration also won a National Book Award. Professor Schlesinger is the Albert Schweitzer Professor of the Humanities at the City University of New York, and has been involved in several other Chelsea House projects, including the REVOLUTIONARY WAR LEADERS and COLONIAL LEADERS series.

Picture Credits